Collaborating
IN THE DIGITAL WORLD

By Anastasia Suen

YOUR
POSITIVE
Digital
Footprint

Author: Anastasia Suen

Series research and development: Reagan Miller

Editors: Janine Deschenes, Reagan Miller,

Proofreader and indexer: Angela Kaelberer

Design, photo research, and prepress:
Margaret Amy Salter

Print coordinator: Katherine Berti

Photo Credits

iStock: front cover, aldomurillo

Shutterstock: p 25, ©Philip Lange

All other images from Shutterstock

Library and Archives Canada Cataloguing in Publication

Suen, Anastasia, author
          Collaborating in the digital world / Anastasia Suen.

(Your positive digital footprint)
Includes index.
Issued in print and electronic formats.
ISBN 978-0-7787-4599-0 (hardcover)
ISBN 978-0-7787-4603-4 (softcover)
ISBN 978-1-4271-2043-4 (HTML)

          1. Social groups--Juvenile literature. 2. Interpersonal
relations--Juvenile literature. 3. Social interaction--Juvenile literature.
4. Cooperativeness--Juvenile literature. 5. Internet--social aspects--
Juvenile literature. I. Title.

HM716.S84 2018   j302.3   C2018-901261-7
                                                                            C2018-901262-5

Library of Congress Cataloging-in-Publication Data

Names: Suen, Anastasia, author.
Title: Collaborating in the digital world / Anastasia Suen.
Description: New York, New York : Crabtree Publishing Company, 2018. |
  Series: Your positive digital footprint | Includes index.
Identifiers: LCCN 2018012557 (print) |
  LCCN 2018016090 (ebook) |
  ISBN 9781427120434 (Electronic) |
  ISBN 9780778745990 (hardcover : alk. paper) |
  ISBN 9780778746034 (pbk. : alk. paper)
Subjects: LCSH: Group work in education. | Education, Cooperative. |
  Computer-assisted instruction.
Classification: LCC LB1032 (ebook) | LCC LB1032 .S845 2018 (print) |
  DDC 371.39/5--dc23
LC record available at https://lccn.loc.gov/2018012557

Crabtree Publishing Company

www.crabtreebooks.com   1-800-387-7650

Printed in the U.S.A./052018/BG20180327

Published in Canada
Crabtree Publishing
616 Welland Ave.
St. Catharines, Ontario
L2M 5V6

Published in the United States
Crabtree Publishing
PMB 59051
350 Fifth Avenue, 59th Floor
New York, New York 10118

Published in the United Kingdom
Crabtree Publishing
Maritime House
Basin Road North, Hove
BN41 1WR

Published in Australia
Crabtree Publishing
3 Charles Street
Coburg North
VIC, 3058

Contents

Collaborating: Then and Now

To **collaborate** means, very simply, to work together with others. People have always known that big projects are difficult to complete without help. Collaborating means that people can bring different ideas, backgrounds, and knowledge together to create something amazing! Although collaboration has likely taken place since the beginning of time, the ways we collaborate are always changing.

Flashback to the Past

Forty years ago, if you wanted to collaborate with a group of friends, you called them on the phone, one by one. Someone else might answer the phone in the kitchen, and yell for your friend to come to the phone. But if your friend wasn't home, you had to hope the person who answered passed on your message. Then you had to wait for them to call you back.

Going back even further, you might have had to send a handwritten letter to arrange a meeting with someone. If your friend lived far away, it could take a week or more for your letter to reach them!

Flash Forward to 2018

To **communicate** with your friends today, you can send them a text. You can also send an email, which is like sending a letter to your whole group—at once! You can collaborate with others face to face on your smartphone by using a video **app**, such as Facetime or Skype.

You can even work together in real time using web programs such as Google Docs. This allows people in different places to work on the same online document at the same time.

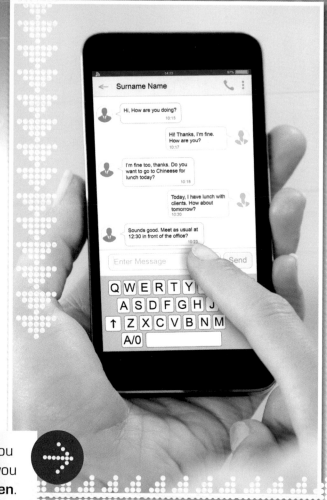

Today, you collaborate in a digital world. You have amazing tools at your disposal—but you also have responsibilities as a **digital citizen**.

TECH TIP

To send the same letter to two friends in 1978, you had two choices. You could write each letter by hand. Or you could place a sheet of **carbon paper** in between the two letters. The carbon paper in the middle would make a copy on the bottom sheet. This was quicker than writing the same letter twice—but it's not even close to the speed of emails.

To send the same letter to two friends today, just add the second name to the cc (carbon copy) line at the top of your email.

How do People Collaborate?

1

The first part is **interpersonal communication**. When you work with others, you need to be able to communicate with them. Good communication requires that you share your ideas with others and show respect for their ideas.

Collaboration is made up of three main elements, or parts.

3

The third part is **task management**. This involves making decisions on how the work will get done. How will you break down the task, or project, into steps or parts? Who will do each part? How much time will each part take? How will you put all of the parts together?

2

Conflict resolution is the second element of collaboration. Some projects don't work as planned. Sometimes group members disagree. It's important to be able to resolve, or fix, these issues when they arise. Conflict resolution means group members talk through a problem, reach an agreement, and take action to overcome it.

What is Collaborating?

Collaborating is not:	Collaborating is:
I do what you say. You do what I say.	I share my ideas. You share your ideas. We listen to each other. We work together. We solve problems together.

You are a Digital Citizen

Using digital tools and devices, you can collaborate with people all around the world. You can reach someone on the other side of the world in seconds. This makes you a citizen of the digital world. You interact, or engage, with other digital citizens, which makes you a part of a **global** community of digital **technology** users. Through your interactions, you have an impact on how others experience digital technology. You have a responsibility to ensure you are a positive contributer to the community.

What does it mean to be a citizen?

You are a citizen of the place where you are born. Your citizenship describes your relationship to others in the world. Being a citizen gives you **rights** and **privileges**—but it also means you have responsibilities to interact safely, collaborate positively, and contribute your ideas.

As an animal lover, you want to create a **blog** post about endangered animals in your region. Using digital communication tools, you can collaborate with young people who live in other cities near you to learn about their **perspectives** on the endangered animals, too! Including many perspectives can support your ideas, help you come up with new ideas, and make your post more interesting.

Digital Citizenship

With new digital technology comes new responsibilities. As a digital citizen, you should always put safety first, respect the laws, and behave in a way that reflects how we would like others to treat us. What you do and say online will be viewed by many people, so make sure you put your best foot forward.

When you share photos on Instagram, send an email, or post a **podcast** recording, you are creating your **digital footprint**. Digital citizenship isn't only about being safe online. It is also about learning how to use the digital tools at your fingertips to contribute your thoughts, ideas, and creative work to the **digital community**. When you collaborate with other digital citizens, you are contributing to the digital community in a meaningful way—and creating a positive digital footprint.

Collaborating to Share Knowledge

For a digital citizen, learning and sharing go together. After you learn something new, you can collaborate online to share it with others. Who said that adults were the only people who could teach?

DIGITAL DYNAMO

LEARN IT
TEACH IT

The Student Tech Team at Burlington High School

If you need help with your computer at Burlington High in Massachusetts, you take it to the Tech Team. Each semester, high school students run their own tech support system at the back of the school library. The Tech Team helps both teachers and students who are having computer issues.

The Student Tech Team also investigates new technologies to share with their peers and teachers! Teachers invite the Tech Team members to give classroom demonstrations of new technologies. Each student on the team also shares their knowledge in a group blog. There are posts about all kinds of technology. New apps are also introduced in these blog posts. The Student Tech Team's goal is to help students, teachers, and parents use new technology.

Share Your Knowledge Online

The teens on the Student Tech Team shared their knowledge on a school blog and on their personal blogs. You can do the same thing. You can share your knowledge online by creating a blog and writing **posts** about the things you are interested in or know how to do. If you are under 13, you must ask an adult to help you.

Why do you need to be 13? There is a law in the United States called the Child Online Privacy Protection Act (COPPA) that protects young people online. Companies online cannot collect any information about people under age 13, so you are not able to sign up for website accounts on your own. To collaborate with anyone online using tools that require accounts, you will need an adult to sign up for you. The same rules are recommended in Canada by the Office of the Privacy Commissioner.

bulb
digital portfolios

TECH TIP

You can set up an online collection folder to show your school work. One app to try is called Bulb. The work that you create in this app will stay in your folder year after year. You can even use it after you graduate!

Collaborating to Teach

Collaborating with others to swap knowledge is a wonderful way to be a positive digital citizen. You are helping others—and receiving help in return when you need it. Sharing or teaching knowledge can take many forms. Google Docs and Google Slides are great ways that you can record and share your knowledge—just type in the email addresses of the people with whom you wish to share. You can even work from different places on the same documents together!

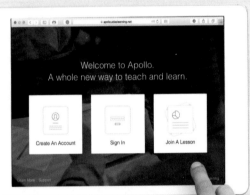

The Apollo app is another way you can share what you know at your school. Write down what you want to share in a document or a slide deck, which is a collection of slides for a presentation. The app will convert your work so everyone can see it. When you're ready to share, open your lesson. The Apollo app will show your work on each person's device in real time. The teacher and the other students can watch your lesson point by point.

Choosing your tool

Which is better: a document or a slide deck? It depends on the content you want to share.

Sharing a document will show your words as you teach step by step. This works well if you can't use any sound. If you share a slide deck, you can show images with short captions. Slides work well if viewers need to see what you are doing. Adding sound to your slide deck will give you a winning combination. The images show what you are doing. The short captions briefly state your ideas. The sound captures all of the details!

As you share your knowledge on Apollo, you can invite the class to collaborate with you! Ask questions, and let each person share their answers with you and the other participants on their devices. You can even record your Apollo lesson so that the work you did together is saved as a video. Everyone can watch and listen to the replay later at home. You can also show off your collaborative teaching and learning to friends and family.

Collaborating to Solve Problems

Digital tools can allow you to work with people in different places to solve problems. Working with people from different places allows you to learn new ideas and see problems from different perspectives. That's what some students in Maryland did for Digital Learning Day in 2017. As they competed in a **Makerspace** challenge, they used **video conferencing** to talk to students in another school.

DIGITAL DYNAMO

Collaborating Across Classrooms

In February 2017, fifth-grade students at Crellin Elementary School watched their computer screens closely. Instructions for their project were being explained in another classroom—somewhere else in the state! Their challenge was to build a catapult with construction paper, scissors, tape, paper clips, and rubber bands. It was going to take collaboration to get the job done. The students worked in small groups in each classroom. Each group also had a computer that connected them with students in the other classroom. The students in both classrooms shared their knowledge and ideas. They collaborated to complete the challenge!

Count the Ways

There were many ways in which the students in both classrooms collaborated. There were two classroom teachers to ask for advice. Students collaborated in their small groups. Different small groups in each classroom also shared ideas with each other. Each small group could also use their computer to ask the group in the other classroom for advice and share their knowledge with them.

How did all of this sharing help the students meet their challenge? Seeing what others did is very helpful. They could also talk over their ideas and try something new. Without the digital tools they used, the project would not have been possible!

Be a Team Player

Do you play team sports, such as soccer, basketball, or lacrosse? You probably know that every team has rules to follow and roles for each player. That way everyone knows what to expect. The same is true with collaboration. The first time you meet with your group, talk about your team rules, roles, and the goals you want to achieve.

Goal

What are you trying to do or achieve together? Take some time to talk over your goal with the group. Write down your ideas and discuss them. Come to an agreement about your group's goal right from the start, and make sure everyone understands your goal in the same way.

Time

How long will your project last? Will you meet once or twice a week? How long will you meet each time? Talk it over with your group to see what works best. Make some rules about what a group member should do if they can't meet. These might include notifying all group members in advance or using a digital tool to attend the meeting **remotely**.

Roles

When you play a sport, each person has a different role. Each role plays a part in helping the team reach its goal.

What are the roles needed in your group? Will you need a team leader, a subject-matter expert, an idea tester, a timekeeper, a note taker, or a scheduler? Discuss what needs to be done and who can do it. Everyone needs to participate.

Keeping Records

How will you keep track of the work your team completes and the work still to be done? How will someone catch up after missing the meeting? You will need to keep records of your collaborative project. How will you create and keep these records? Will each person make their own notes? Will you save all of your work in one place?

Communication Checklist

Communication is an essential part of working with others. When you collaborate, you will spend a lot of time talking. To work together as a group, you must find a way to agree on what to do each step of the way. You must also communicate effectively, so that every person clearly understands the group's rules, roles, and goals.

Projects sometimes move in unexpected directions or can suddenly be faced with new challenges. The good news about dealing with unexpected challenges during a collaborative project is that you have all of the other members of the group to help you.

Use these steps in this checklist to guide your discussions when problems arise.

☐ **Name the problem:** Introduce the new problem to the group.

☐ **Share experiences:** Ask group members to share what they did about this problem in the past.

☐ **Brainstorm new ideas:** Make a list of possible ways to solve the problem.

☐ **Narrow down the list:** Cross off choices that won't work right now.

☐ **Compare the choices:** Make a pros-and-cons list for each of your final choices.

☐ **Reach an agreement:** Make a group decision about what to do next.

A Lifelong Skill

Collaborating with a group is a skill that has to be learned. It can be hard to listen to people who have very different ideas than you have. Learning to collaborate is a lifelong process!

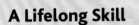

The secret to effective communication is respect. You don't have to agree with someone, but you have to listen to their ideas and let them speak without interruption. Don't use **body language** to disagree, either. Picture how it feels when someone rolls their eyes, shakes their head, or sighs when you talk. This body language does not show that they are listening to you or respecting your ideas. Treat the other members of your group the way you would want to be treated.

Break it Down

Tackling a big project can be challenging! It can be hard to coordinate with others to get things done. Make collaboration projects easier by using digital tools to break big projects into small steps.

To stay organized and keep track of finished and incomplete work, you can upload all of your work in one digital file. Uploading means to send your file from one computer to another or to a network to share with others. As soon each person does their work, upload it to the shared file. Save all of your group work there.

Make a Kanban Board

A kanban board is like a whiteboard showing a chart with three columns. It is used to help break down a project and assign each part to different people. First you must make a list of each and every task that needs to be done for your project.

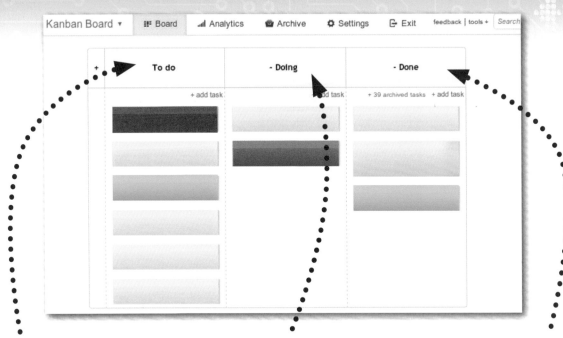

A kanban board has three columns. The first column is labeled "To Do." It lists every part of your project that still needs to be done.

The middle column is labeled "Doing." When you begin working on a task, move it from the first column to the middle column. Then add your name to the task.

The third column is labeled "Done." After you finish your task, move it here.

Google docs

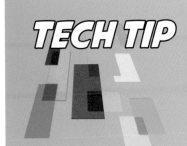

Invite each person in the group to a shared workspace online. You can use a shared website, called a **wiki**, or subscribe to shared **software** such as Office 365 or Google Docs. You can build your kanban board online where everyone in the group can see it.

Managing Tasks

Break each task into small steps that can be distributed among members to complete by the next meeting. You can use a calendar app to create a group calendar. The group calendar can send reminders to each member when their task deadline is approaching. Set the reminder as many days in advance as you like.

Talk about your tasks at each group meeting. Discuss what you did. Add any new tasks to your kanban board. Ask for help if you need it. Talk about what needs to happen next. End each group meeting with a decision about what each person will do next. Be specific and set clear deadlines. Then add the new deadlines into your calendar.

To Do List

Now that you know what to do, which day will you do it? Use an app to make a "To Do" list for yourself.

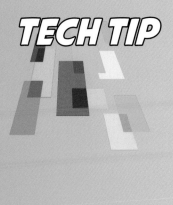

TECH TIP

If your group is using Google, you can make a "To Do" list in your email. Open your email and click on the upper left side of the screen. The word "Tasks" will show up under the words "Contacts" and "Gmail." Click on the word "Tasks" and a box will open on the lower left. Add your tasks and make lists.

If your group is using Office 365, download the Microsoft To-Do List app. Then make a list of all of your "To Dos." Each day, the app will review your "To Do" lists. It will add what it thinks you need to do to your "My Day" list. Apps like these will help you plan your day!

Think Globally Act Locally

You don't have to travel very far to get involved in the global community. You can be a digital citizen in your own neighborhood. You can start at school. That's how more than five million students around the world have shared their work. They collaborate in the International CyberFair.

INTERNATIONAL SCHOOLS CYBERFAIR SHARE & UNITE

The vision is . . . Inspire and Unite!

A Year of Collaboration

This project lasts the entire school year. Each October, the CyberFair announces a new theme, or subject, for the projects. The theme is broken into eight categories, or more specific topics. To participate, you will need a teacher to **sponsor** you.

Choosing Your Topic

After you form your small group, choose a category together. You have six months to complete your research. Use **social media** to find people in your community who might help you with your topic. Your group will use its research to build a website. You will need to test it for bugs before you let everyone else see it.

Peer Review

All the websites are reviewed in April by other students. This is called peer review. Every group is given a set of instructions on how to evaluate each website. Your group will review the work of six other groups from around the globe.

In May, the students' top choices in each category go to a panel of judges. Finalists in each category will be posted on the CyberFair webpage. Experts from around the world will review the projects. Then the winners are announced!

DIGITAL DYNAMO

2017 International CyberFair Finalists

Where you live will help you decide what to study. Two of the 2017 winners provide a clear example. One group of students live in a large city—Kowloon, Hong Kong. They studied how people used escalators to travel to and from the subway trains. The students in Hsichou Township, Taiwan, live in a rural area. They studied how crops grow.

Reaching Your Goals

Knowing where you want to go will help you get there. Each step of the way, think about your goal. What do you want to accomplish with this project? Is the work you are doing leading to your goal?

DIGITAL DYNAMO

The Massage Rope Team

ePals is an online community of teachers and students from around the world. They share activities, collaborate on projects, and learn about each other's cultures. Every year, ePals holds its Invent It! Challenge. In 2016, the students were challenged to think of a real-world health problem and come up with a solution. A group of five students from New Jersey, who were also athletes, won in their category. How did they do it?

STEP 1

Identify a Problem

The first step in a problem-solving project is to identify a problem. The ten- and eleven-year-olds in this group used their own experiences with sports injuries. They decided to invent something to help athletes stay fit while they recovered from a leg injury.

STEP 2

Research

After you name the problem, look around to see what others have done to solve this problem. That's what these five students did. They found out what others did. Then they figured out a way to add their own ideas. They used the **SCAMPER** thinking method.

- **S**ubstitute ◀ ·········
- **C**ombine
- **A**dd
- **M**inimize, or Maximize, or Modify
- **P**ut it to another use
- **E**liminate Something
- **R**earrange or Reverse

STEP 3

Sketches

The next step is to make drawings of the ideas. These students drew what their **invention** might look like. They added notes to show how it worked. These drawings helped them decide which ideas they wanted to try to build. More drawings followed!

STEP 4

Make a Prototype

Bringing the drawings to life is the next step. The students made three models, called **prototypes**, based on their drawings. They had to make decisions about which materials to use. They also had to decide which prototype worked best. Which one did what they wanted it to do?

Asking for Help

After they built their prototype, the students had something to show for all of their hard work. It might seem like they were done at this point, but their project wasn't finished yet. Building a prototype is not the end of the invention process. After you build something, you have to see if it really works! The best way to do that is to ask others to try it and tell you what they think.

STEP 5

Testing and Feedback
After the students selected the best prototype, they tested it. Then they asked others to test it, too. After each test, the students listened to what the others had to say. This is called feedback. They wanted their opinions so they could improve their invention.

STEP 6

The Finished Product
The students made improvements to their invention using the feedback from all of their tests. It was finally time to make the finished product—the Massage Rope!

Telling the Story

Once the invention was completed, it was time to share their idea with others. The students made a video that told the story of their invention from idea to finished product. Why did they do that? (See their video here: https://bit.ly/2ur97SQ)

To win the competition, the students also had to "sell" everyone on their invention. Visitors to their webpage who liked their idea "paid" with their votes, not money. Over 1.9 million people voted in the 2016 contest. The kids from New Jersey and their Massage Rope won in their category!

Now It's Your Turn

Collaborating with others is a great way to get things done. When you work as a team, you can accomplish amazing things. Using digital tools allows you to collaborate with people near and far. You can work with other students in your class. You can work with students on the other side of the globe. Why not? You are a digital citizen!

Glossary

app A small computer program, such as a game, downloaded and used on mobile devices such as tablets and smartphones

blog Short for web log, a list of journal entries posted on a web page for others to read

body language Movements or positions of the body that show a person's thoughts or feelings

brainstorm To quickly come up with and record lots of ideas without judging them

carbon paper Thin paper coated in carbon, a material formed after something is burned

collaborate To work together with one or more people

communicate To share thoughts, ideas, and feelings

digital citizen A person who uses computer technology

digital community People who interact through the Internet or digital platforms

digital footprint A record of all the things you do online

global Relating to the entire world

interpersonal Between people

invention A product that did not previously exist

Makerspace A place where learning is encouraged through hands-on activity and creative problem solving

media A means of communication, such as the Internet

perspectives Viewpoints

podcast A series of sound files that others listen to

posts Messages regularly published online

privileges Advantages given to certain people

prototype An experimental model of an invention

remotely From a distance

rights The things that people are legally able to do or have

SCAMPER A method of thinking in new ways by reworking information; the name is formed by the first letters of seven action words.

social media Websites and applications that let you create and share content

software The program used to give directions to a digital device

sponsor Take responsibility for

task management The planning, organizing, and directing on how the work will get done

technology A use of scientific knowledge to solve problems

video conferencing Holding a meeting over the Internet in which members in different places can see one another onscreen

wiki A website that allows anyone to add, delete, or revise content